Night Flight

LEVEL 4

/igh/
/ur/

DECODABLES BY jump!

Teaching Tips

Blue Level 4

This book focuses on the phonemes **/igh/ur/**.

Before Reading

- Discuss the title. Ask readers what they think the book will be about. Have them briefly explain why.
- Ask readers to sort the words on page 3. Read the sounds and words together.

Read the Book

- Encourage readers to break down unfamiliar words into units of sound. Then, ask them to string the sounds together to create the words.
- Urge readers to point out when the focused phonics phonemes appear in the text.

After Reading

- Encourage children to reread the book independently or with a friend.
- Ask readers to name other words with /igh/ or /ur/ phonemes. On a separate sheet of paper, have them write the words out.

5357 Penn Avenue South
Minneapolis, MN 55419
www.jumplibrary.com

Decodables by Jump! are published by Jump! Library.

Library of Congress Cataloging-in-Publication Data is available at www.loc.gov or upon request from the publisher.

ISBN: 979-8-88996-828-3 (hardcover)
ISBN: 979-8-88996-829-0 (paperback)
ISBN: 979-8-88996-830-6 (ebook)

Photo Credits

Images are courtesy of Shutterstock.com. With thanks to Getty Images, Thinkstock Photo and iStockphoto. Cover – CGi Heart. 4–5 – Frame Stock Footage, David Pereiras. 6–7 – Quisquilia, Kichigin. 8–9 – Jack Frog, Jens Goepfert. 10–11 – sebastianosecondi, Volar sin Parar. 12–13 – Guido Benedetto, Leonardo da. 14–15 – Deyan Georgiev, Zurijeta. 16 – Shutterstock.

Can you sort all the words on this page into two groups?

Fur

Right

Words with
igh

Light

Turn

Surf

Sight

Might

Words with
ur

Burn

Curb

Night

They are going on a trip. They must get on a flight at midnight.

They will need to rush. They might miss the flight. They must rush to the van.

They need to get the bags in the back of the van.

They will need to go in the van to get to the jet.

They look for a spot to park the van.
They look left and right.

They park the van next to the curb.
Then they get the bags out.

They must find the check-in desk.
They can turn the bags in there.

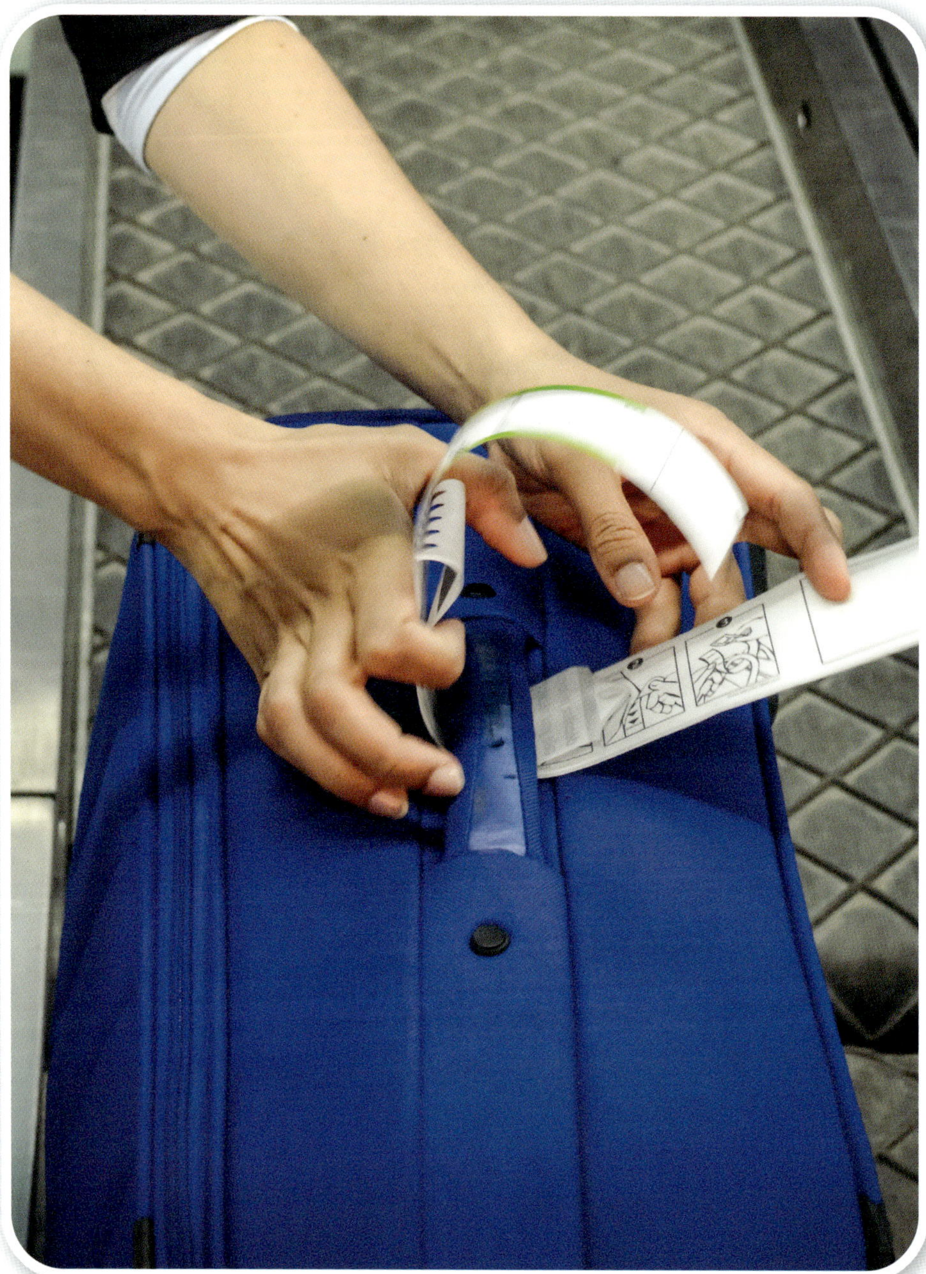

It is midnight. Now they must get on the jet.

The jet starts up. They feel a lurch as it turns right.

There is a big woosh as the jet takes off.

The jet is up high. They can see lots of lights at night.

The flight will be long. They all curl up and sleep for the night.

Sound out each word. Does it have an /igh/ or /ur/ sound?

light

nurse

knight

purple